Piano for Everyone - Level One
ISBN: 978-1-897515-08-2
AP-5040

Copyright 2007 Alethia Publications.
Printed in Canada.

Table of Contents

Chapter 1
PIANO BASICS

Overview
• learning note names on piano keyboard
• learning proper hand/finger placement
• reading bass and treble clef notes
• reading and playing left and right hands on grand staff

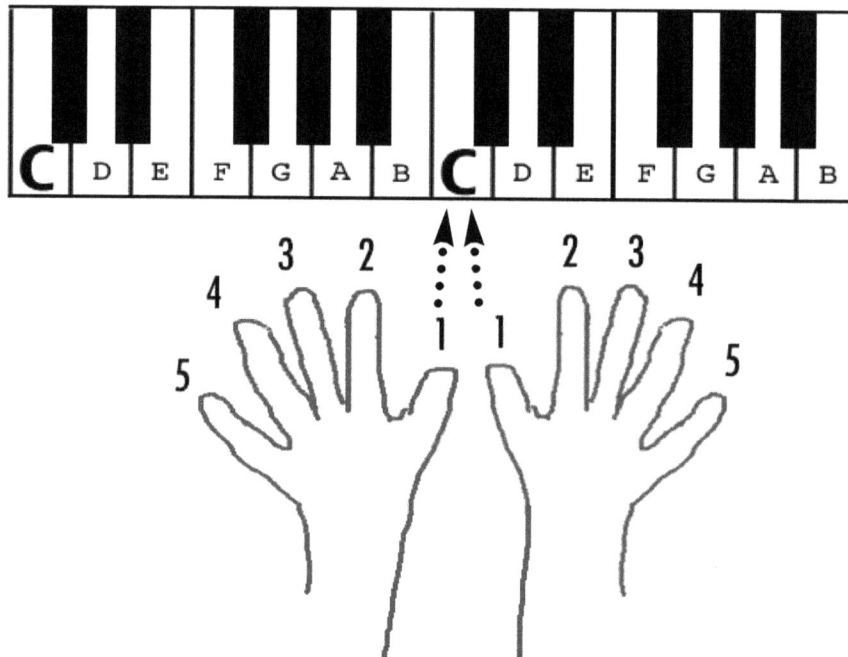

Matching Fingers to the Keyboard

Right Hand:

1.) Using the above figures as a reference, with your hand in a rounded position, place your right thumb on middle C/Doh on the keyboard. Play the C/Doh with your right thumb a few times in a steady, even rhythm.

2.) The right index finger (2) should be resting on D/Re, along with the other right hand fingers and their corresponding notes. Try playing each of the notes (C-D-E-F-G) with the appropriate finger in an steady, even rhythm.

Left Hand:

2.) Using the above figures as a reference, with your hand in a rounded position, place your left thumb on middle C/Doh on the keyboard. Play the C/Doh with your left thumb a few times in an even rhythm.

The left index finger (2) should be resting on B/Si, along with the other left hand fingers and their corresponding notes. Try playing each of the notes (C-B-A-G-F) in the left hand with the appropriate finger in an even, steady rhythm.

•Remember to keep both hands in a rounded position •

1

1.1 - MATCHING FINGERS WITH NOTATION

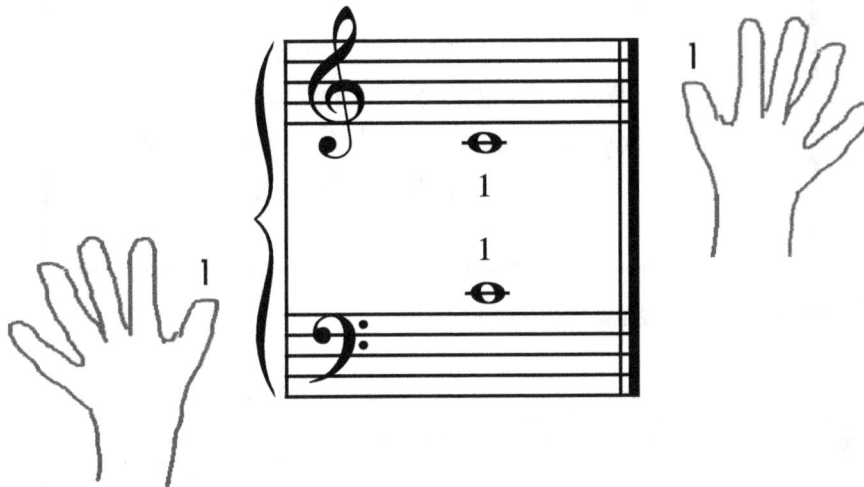

Getting Started...

Step One:

Using the above illustration, match your right hand thumb (1) to the 1 on the treble clef (top clef) on the grand staff. Play the note for four steady counts.

Step Two:

With your left hand, match your left thumb (1) to the 1 on the bass clef (bottom clef) on the grand staff. Play the note for four steady counts.

Step Three:

Now, try the exercise as written on the grand staff below. (It should sound the same as Step One and Two.)

1.2 - ADDING MORE RHYTHMS

This is a half note.
We play a half note for two beats, or pulses.
Say "1-2" for the first half note and "3-4" for
the second half note in each measure.

EXERCISE: Play the exercise below using the correct rhythms.

1.2a

"1-2"   "1-2"   "1-2-3-4"

"3-4"   "3-4"   "1-2-3-4"

This is a quarter note.
We play a quarter note for one beat, or pulse.
Say "1" for the first quarter note, "2" for
the second quarter note and so on in each measure.

EXERCISE: Play the exercise below using the correct rhythms.

1.2b

"1"   "3"   "1-2"   "1-2-3-4"

"2"   "4"   "3-4"   "1-2-3-4"

1.3 - ADDING MORE NOTES

EXERCISE: Play the exercises below using the correct rhythms.

1.3a

"1-2" "3-4"   "1-2-3-4"

"1-2" "3-4"   "1-2-3-4"

1.3b

"1" "2"   "1" "2" "3-4"   "3" "4"

"3" "4"   "1" "2"   "1" "2" "3-4"

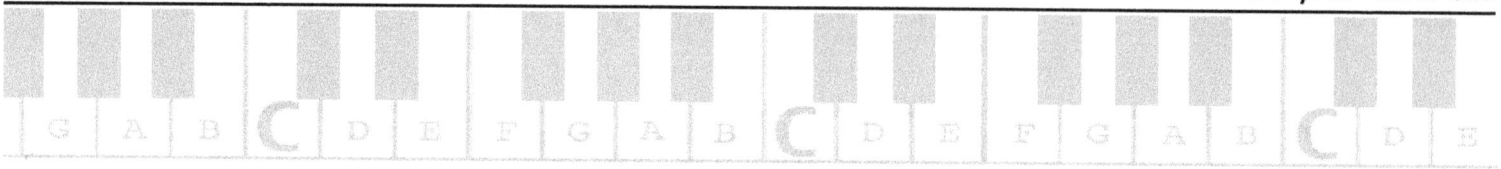

EXERCISE: Play the exercises below using the correct rhythms.

Remember: Use your correct fingering - start with your thumbs on middle C.

1.3c

"1-2-3-4"

"1-2-3-4"

1.3d

"1-2"

"3-4"

"3-4"

"1-2"

Use the fingering hints!

1.4 - REVIEW EXERCISES

a.

b.

c.

CHALLENGE EXERCISES: Playing with both hands together

d.

e.

Chapter 2
MORE BASICS

Overview
- writing in fingerings
- playing with both hands
- introduction of C, Ds and E in left hand

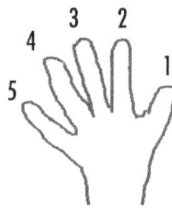

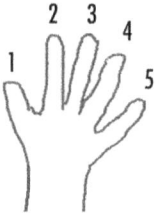

2.1 - FINGERING REVIEW

EXERCISE: Write the fingerings for each note on the lines below. Play each exercise.

2.1a

"1-2" "3-4"

"1-2-3-4"

2.1b

"1-2-3-4"

"1-2-3-4"

2.2 - PLAYING BOTH HANDS TOGETHER

Step One: Play each hand separately, counting carefully.

Step Two: Play with two hands together.

Write in the fingerings!

EXERCISE: Play each hand separately, then play with hands together.

2.2a

"1-2-3-4"

2.2b

2.2c

2.3 - NEW NOTES IN THE LEFT HAND

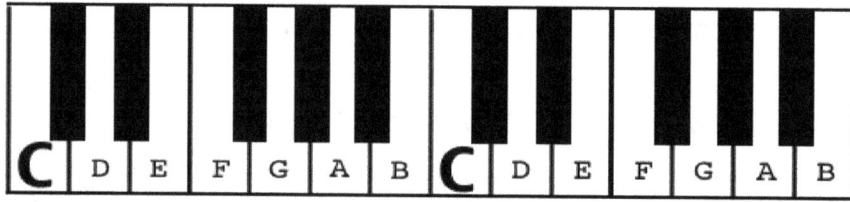

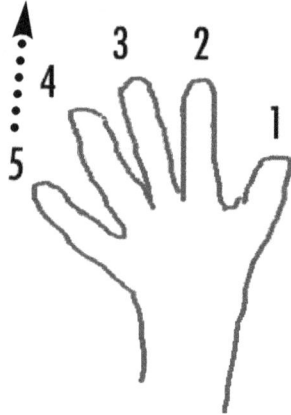

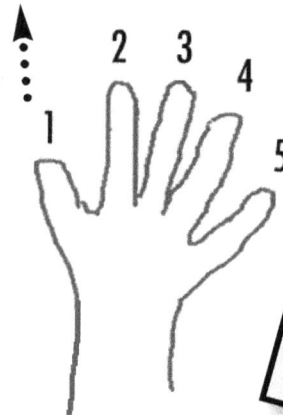

To play the lower notes in the left hand, reposition your hand so that your thumb (1) is on the G below middle C.

EXERCISE: Write in the notes and fingerings for the left hand, then play each exercise.

2.3a

2.3b

9

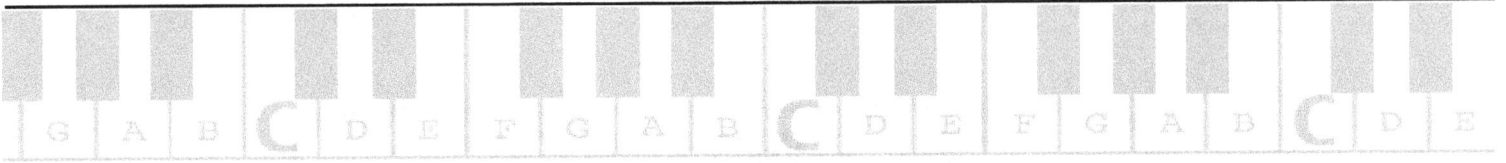

2.3c

New Note: D/Re
Sometimes, we need to shift our hand
position to play higher notes.
Take note of the fingering changes.

EXERCISE: Play each hand separately, then play hands together.

2.3d

5   4   3   1   2   New note D/Re

2.3e

5   4   1

2.4 - REVIEW EXERCISES

Write in fingering hints!

EXERCISES: In the following exercises, play each hand separately, then play with hands together. Keep a steady tempo (speed) and use the appropriate fingerings.

e.

Always look ahead...
Look ahead a few notes so you can prepare
for a shift in your hand position. Don't forget to
write in the fingerings where necessary

CHALLENGE EXERCISES: Play each hand separately, then play together.

c.

d.

"1" "2" "3" | "1" "2" "3" | "1" "2" "3" | "1-2-3" | "1" "2" "3" | "1" "2" "3" | "1" "2" "3" | "1-2-3"

e.

3

www.thevirtualschoolofmusic.com

2.5 - MUSIC IN PRACTICE

Joyful, Joyful
from the 9th Symphony

composed by Ludwig van Beethoven
Variation I, arranged by C.A. Johnson

Chapter 3
MORE NOTES

Overview
- new notes in right hand
  - A, B, C, D and Bb
- new notes in left hand
  - B, Bb, A and G

G   A   B   C   D

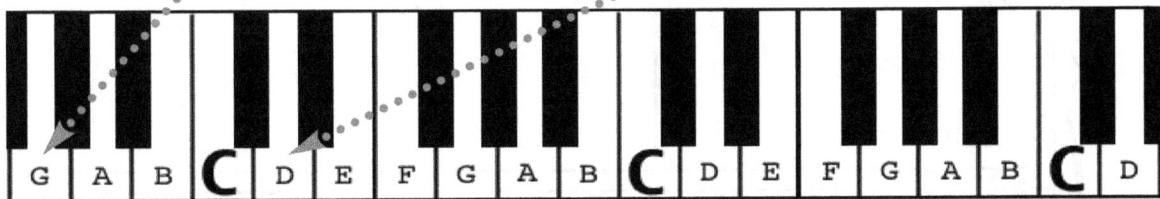

3.1 - INTRODUCING NEW NOTES

Use the suggested fingerings

3.2 - INTRODUCING D

3.3 - NEW NOTE Bb

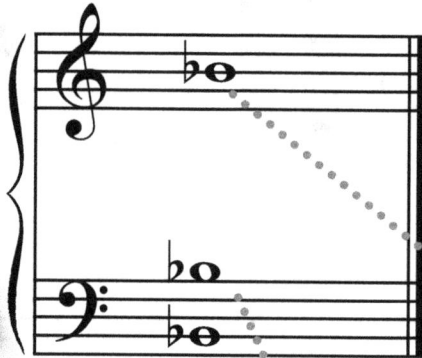

FLAT SIGNS
The flat sign means that the pitch is a HALF step LOWER in sound than the regular pitch. On the piano, Bb is found in between B and A.

About Bb...
We say "B-flat" but is it written with the flat sign BEFORE the note.

3.3a

3.3b

3.4 - REVIEW EXERCISES

EXERCISE: In the following exercises, play each hand separately, then play with hands together. Keep a steady tempo (speed) and use the appropriate fingerings.

a.

b.

Be prepared for Bbs!

c.

d.

Chapter 4 TWO-NOTE CHORDS

4.1 - CHORD FINGERINGS

Chord Fingerings
Chord Fingerings are written as numbers on top of each other respective to the stacking of notes. For example, in exercise 4.1a, the final chord in the right hand has the thumb (1) play the "E" and the fifth finger (5) play the "C."

Step One:
Read through the music to anticipate hand position and correct fingerings.

Step Two:
Play each hand separately.

Step Three:
Play both hands together.

EXERCISE: Using the method above, play each exercise below.

4.1a

4.2 - MORE TWO-CHORD EXERCISES

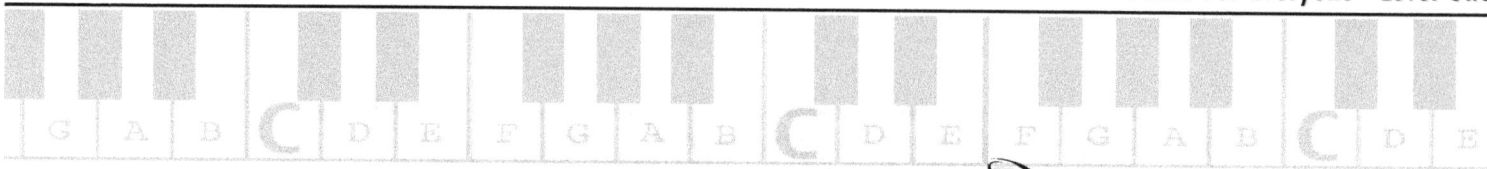

Counting Rhythm

Be sure to count **one** beat for each

♩ (quarter note) and

𝄽 (quarter rest).

4.2e

"1" (2) "3" (4)

4.2f

"1 - 2" "3" (4)

4.2g

21

4.3 - REVIEW EXERCISES

EXERCISES: In the following exercises, play each hand separately, then play with hands together. Keep a steady tempo (speed) and use the appropriate fingerings.

Challenge: New note - F#!

4.4 - A BIT OF MUSIC THEORY

Naturals, Flats and Sharps

When a pitch does not have a symbol infront of it, we say that the pitch is in its **natural form**. When you look at a piano keyboard, the natural notes include only the white keys. The white notes are C - D - E - F - G - A - B - C as displayed below.

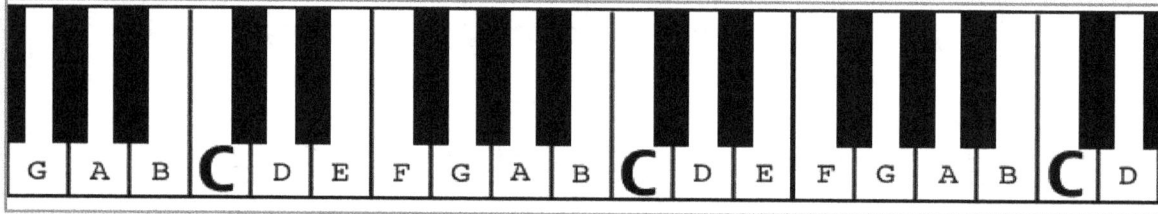

The keyboard is made up of a cycle of 12 half steps. Observe the black notes in between some of the white notes. Now, count the 12 half steps starting at C and move up to finish on C. This pattern of white and black keys is repeated once you reach C again. Look at half step between E and F and B and C. Between these two groupings of white notes there is no black note.

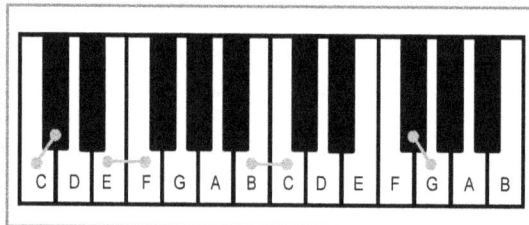

In order to name the black notes, we must adapt the note names by using symbols called accidentals. The flat sign (b) tells the musician that the note is a half step lower than its natural form. On the keyboard below, you can see how each black note uses the note name to its right and then adds the accidental.

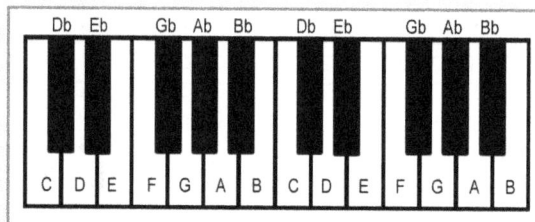

When writing music on a staff, the accidental appears BEFORE the note, centered around the line or space. For example, we would write Bb (say "B-flat") but the note appears like this on a staff:

23

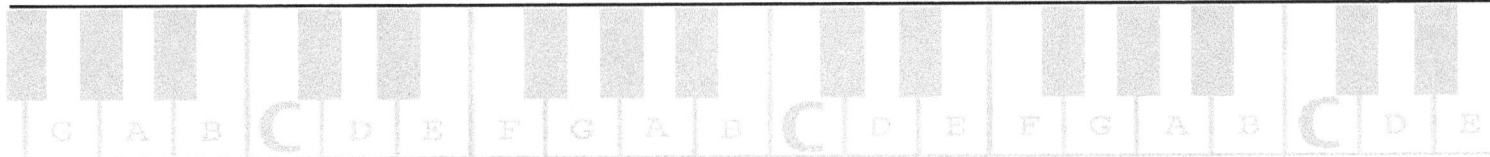

The **sharp** sign (#) tells the musician that the note is a half step higher than its natural form. On the keyboard below, you can see how each black note uses the note name to its left and then adds the sharp accidental.

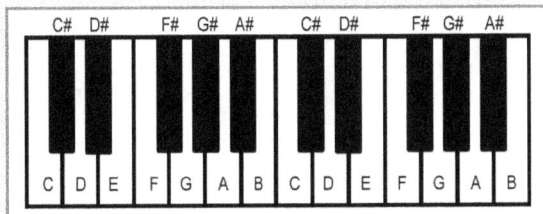

Just like the other accidentals, when we write the sharp accidental on the staff, the sharp is written BEFORE the note.

When speaking of sharped notes, the word "sharp" comes after the letter name, as in F sharp. However, in written music, the sharp sign comes before the note and it is centered with that note regardless if it is on a line or space:

Exercise 1. In this exercise, write flat signs before each note, then name the notes below:

Exercise 2. In this exercise, write sharp signs before each note, then name the notes below:

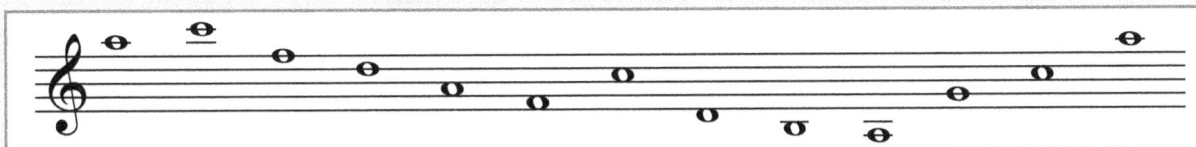

The **natural sign** before a note on the staff, cancels a previous sharp or flat. The natural sign is the same pitch as the **natural form**. Remember that when speaking of natural notes, we say the word "natural" AFTER the letter name (as in "A natural"), however, in written music, the natural sign comes BEFORE the note. In the example below, observe how the natural sign must come BEFORE the second E note. The natural sign cancels the previous flat in the measure.

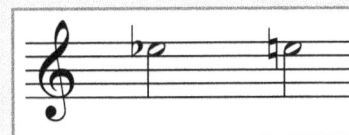

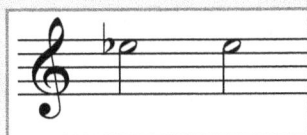

An accidental sign affects the notes written on the same line or space <u>for that measure only</u>. A bar line cancels all accidentals in the previous measure. In the example below, there is no need to write another flat beside the second E note because of the Eb in the earlier part of the measure .

24

4.5 - MUSIC IN PRACTICE

Joyful, Joyful
from the 9th Symphony

composed by Ludwig van Beethoven
Variation II, arranged by C.A. Johnson

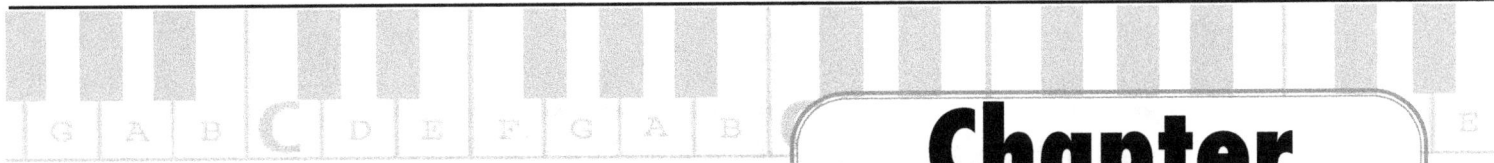

Chapter 5 CREATING THREE-NOTE CHORDS

Overview
- melody and harmony definitions
- playing three-note chords
- learning how to create three-note chords to accompany a right hand melody part (in root position)
- learning more about rhythm

Melody and Harmony

The **melody** of a song can be found in the highest notes of a piano piece. (Generally, the melody is found in the right hand. The melody notes are highlighted with squares in the music below.

The **harmony** of a song is made up of all of the other notes that are not part of the melody. Harmony can be found in the left hand. The harmony part is in marked by the circles in the music below.

Excerpt of theme from Lugwig van Beethoven's Hymn to Joy from the 9th Symphony

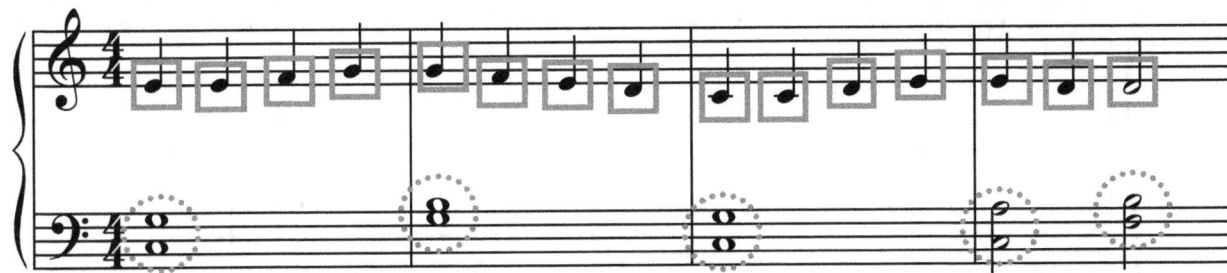

5.1 - PLAYING THREE-NOTE CHORDS

EXERCISES: Play the following three-note chord exercises. Play the right hand separatel and listen to the melody. Then play the left hand separately and listen to the harmony.

5.1a

5.1b

5.1c

5.2 - MORE PRACTICE

Remember to listen for the melody as you are playing each exercise.

EXERCISE: Play the following three-note chord exercises:

5.2a

5.2b

5.2c

5.3 - CREATING THREE-NOTE CHORDS

The melody notes found in the "Joyful, Joyful," by Lugwid van Beethoven (Chapter 4) are found in the following C major scale pattern of notes. Every note in the scale has at least one three-note chord that is related to each note. We call this basic chord a **root position chord**.

EXERCISE: Fill in the other two notes <u>above</u> the lowest note in the root position chord by using the root position chord diagram above to complete exercises 5.3a and 5.3b. (The LOWEST note for each chord is completed for you.)

29

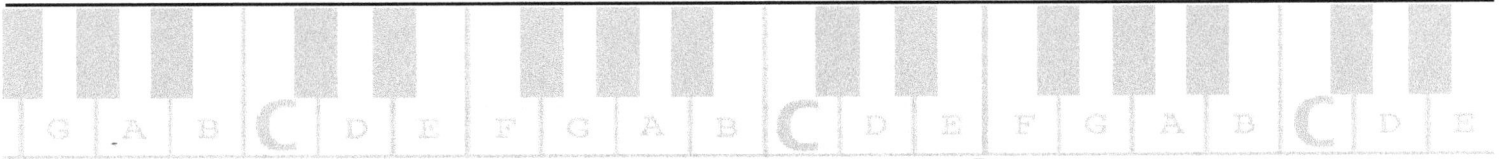

Remember:
Use the chord diagram guide on page 29 to
complete the three-note chord tones
in the left hand.

5.3b

5.3b EXERCISE: Play through exercise 5.3a and 5.3b with the completed three-note chords.

MY NOTES ON THREE-NOTE CHORDS

5.4 - COMPLETING CHORDS TO A SONG

Completing the Chords to a Song:

Now, we are ready to write three-note chords for part of a song that we have already played with two-note chords, Hymn to Joy. In this exercise, the note written in the bass clef is the LOWEST note (or, "**root position**") of the three-note chord.

Use the chord diagram chart on page29 to help you complete each three-note chord in the bass clef.

Joyful, Joyful
from the 9th Symphony

composed by Ludwig van Beethoven

5.4

5.5 - LEARNING MORE ABOUT RHYTHM

The Rhythm Tree of Notes

The Rhythm Tree of Notes shows the value of each note. For example, using the chart below you can see that two half notes are equal to one whole note, and eight eighth notes are equal to one whole note.

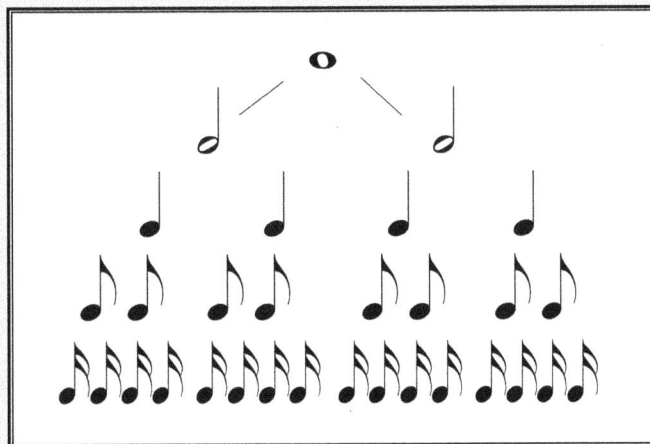

Rests

Just like there are music symbols that tell the musicians how long they are to play a note, there are music symbols that tell the musician how long to **not** play any pitch.

A **Whole Rest** means to rest for a whole measure. It hangs down from the 4th line.
An easy way to remember a whole rest is that it is "heavier" and sinks below the line.

A **Half Rest** is equal to half of a whole rest. It sits on the 3rd line.

A **Quarter Rest** is equal to one quarter of a whole rest. It resembles the letter z in the English alphabet.

An **Eighth Rest** is equal to 1/8th of a whole rest. It resembles the number 7.

There are occasions when the duration of a note cannot be notated using one of the note symbols in the rhythm tree. When this occurs, ties or dots are used.

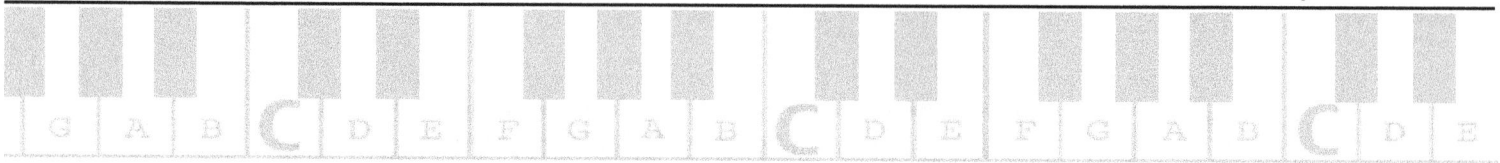

Dotted Notes

A **dot**, placed to the immediate right of the note-head, increases the note's time-value by half. If the note head is located in a space, the dot is placed in that same space. If the note head is on a line, the dot is placed in the space just above the line.

A half note is twice a long in duration than a quarter note. Because a dot following a half note increases its duration by half, a doted half note has the value of 3 quarter notes. In other words, a dotted half note equals an half note plus a quarter note.

Because a dot following a quarter note <u>increases</u> its duration by a 1/2 of a quarter note, a dotted quarter note has a value of 1 and 1/2 quarter notes. In other words, a dotted quarter note equals a quarter note plus an eighth note.

a.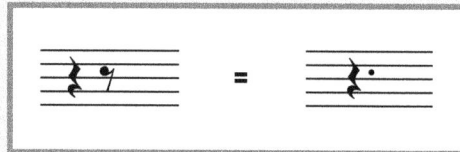

b.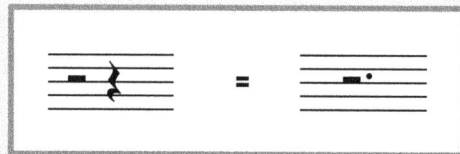

33

Overview
- playing three-note chords: root position and first inversion
- writing three-note chords in first inversion

Chapter 6
FIRST INVERSION CHORDS

Chord Inversions

In the diagram below, we have two more variations (inversions) of the three-note chord that we played in Chapter 5. Play each chord below. The new chords sound very similar to their **root position chord** (R) because they are <u>inversions of the root position chord</u>. (**Inversion** means change of order.)

The first chord (R) is the **root position chord**.

The second chord (1st) is called a **first inversion chord**. The <u>lowest</u> note in the first inversion chord is the second note of the root position chord.

The third chord (2nd) is called a **second inversion chord**. The <u>lowest</u> note of the chord is the third note of the root position chord.

Root Position	First Inversion	Second Inversion
R	1st	2nd

6.1 - PLAYING FIRST INVERSION CHORDS

EXERCISE: Play the following root (R) and first inversion chords (1st):

Listen to the similar sound in the chord inversions.

EXERCISE: Play the following mixtures of root (R) and first inversion chords (1st):

35

6.2 - WRITING FIRST INVERSION CHORDS

Chords provide many harmonic choices for a melody note. The chord diagram below shows the melody notes in the right hand and the root position chord (R) followed by its first inversion chord (1st) in the left hand. Use the diagram to complete the exercises in the following pages.

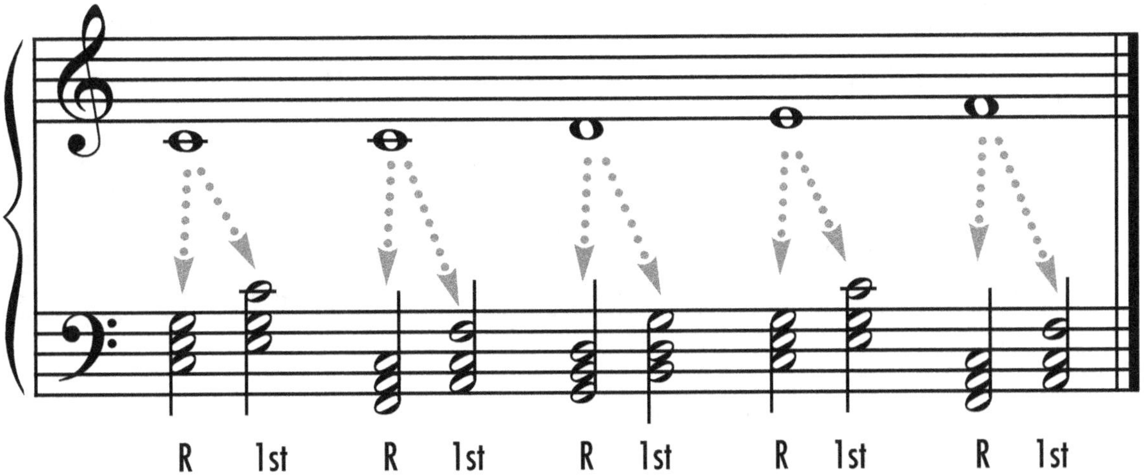

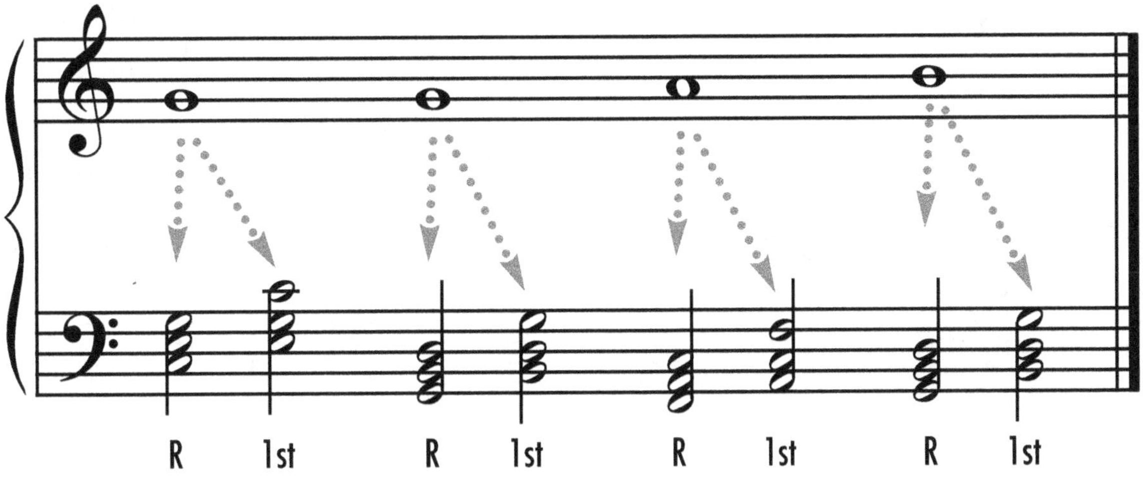

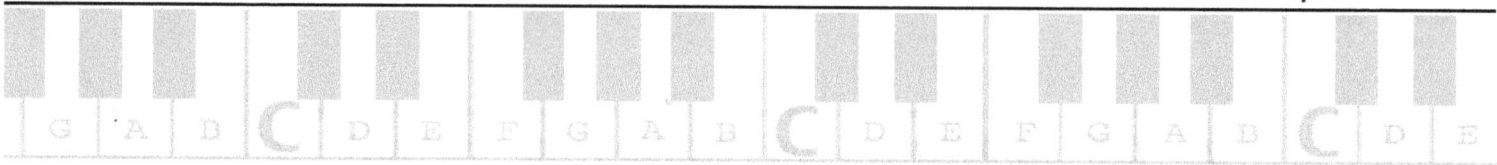

EXERCISE: Write out, then play the following mixtures of root (R) and first inversion chords (1st):

6.2a

1st   1st 1st   1st   1st   1st   1st 1st   R

6.2b

1st   1st   1st   1st   1st   1st   R R R

EXERCISE: Write out, then play the following mixtures of root (A) and first inversion chords (B):

6.2c

R R 1st   R R 1st   R R 1st   1st 1st R

6.3 - COMPLETING CHORDS TO A SONG

Adding Root and First Inversion Chords:

Let's continue to add three-note chords to, "Joyful, Joyful." In this exercise, the "R" below the bass note signifies the root position chord and the "1st" below the bass note signifies a first inversion chord.

Use the **first inversion chord diagram chart** on page 36 to help you complete each three-note chord in the bass clef.

Remember:
A dot behind a note means to hold it one and a half times longer than a note without a dot.

6.3

Joyful, Joyful
from the 9th Symphony

composed by Ludwig van Beethoven

6.4 - MORE EXERCISES

EXERCISE: Using the melody as a guide, determine which chords should be root position and which chords should be first inversion chords. Write in the notes to each left hand chord, then play each exercise.

6.4a

6.4b

6.4c

Overview
• playing second inversion chords
• writing second inversion chords

Chapter 7
2nd INVERSION CHORDS

GETTING STARTED...

Recall that chords can be played in various positions on the piano.
Here we have the **3 types of chord positions** found in harmony:
root position (R), **first inversion** (1st Inv.), and **second inversion** (2nd Inv.).

This chapter will focus on playing and writing second inversion chords.

Root	1st Inv.	2nd Inv.
Root Position	First Inversion	Second Inversion

7.1 - PLAYING SECOND INVERSION CHORDS

EXERCISE: Play the following root (R) and second inversion chords (2nd):

7.1a

R   2nd   R   2nd   R   2nd   R

7.1b

R   2nd 2nd   R   2nd 2nd   R   2nd   R

EXERCISE: Play the following mixtures of root (R), first inversion (1st) and second inversion chords (2nd):

7.1c

2nd   1st   R   1st   2nd   2nd 1st   R

41

7.2 - WRITING SECOND INVERSION CHORDS

Recall from Chapter 6 that chords provide harmonic choices for a melody note. Our final chord diagram, pictured below, shows the melody notes in the right hand, with the **root position chord (R)** followed by its **first inversion chord (1st)**, and **second inversion chord (2nd)** in the left hand. Use this diagram to complete the exercises in the following pages.

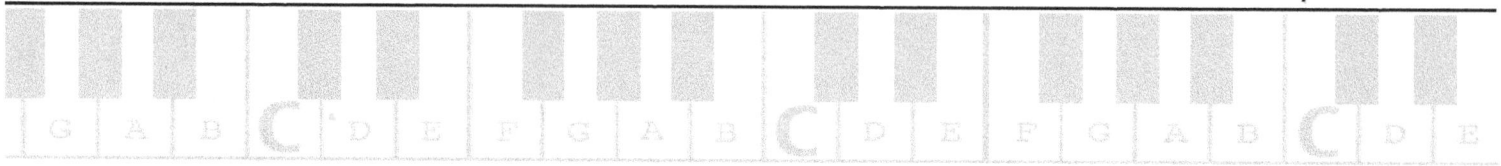

EXERCISE: Write out, then play the following second inversion chords (2nd):

7.2a

2nd   2nd   2nd   2nd

7.2b

2nd   2nd   2nd   2nd   2nd   2nd

EXERCISE: Write out, then play the following mixtures of root (R), and second inversion chords (2nd):

7.2c

2nd   R   2nd   R   2nd   R   2nd   R

7.3 - COMPLETING CHORDS TO A SONG

Using Root, First Inversion and Second Inversion Chords:

Let's use our knowledge of chord inversions to write the left hand harmony for, "Joyful, Joyful." In this exercise, the "R" below the bass note signifies the root position chord, the "1st" below the bass note signifies a first inversion chord, and the "2nd" signifies a second inversion chord.

Use the **second inversion chord diagram chart** on page** to help you complete each three-note chord in the bass clef.

Joyful, Joyful
from the 9th Symphony

composed by Ludwig van Beethoven

R   1st   2nd   R   1st   R   1st   2nd   R   R   2nd   1st   R   1st   R

R   1st   2nd   1st   R   1st   2nd   R   2nd   R   2nd   1st   R   2nd   R

7.4 - MORE PLAYING PRACTICE

EXERCISE: Play the following three-note chord exercises. (Listen for the inversions while you play.):

7.4a

7.4b

7.4c

Chapter 8 NEW KEYS

Overview
- learning chords in the key of F and G
- playing chords using letters
- writing chords using letters

In the past chapters, we used the **key of C** as our learning model. Now, let's use the keys of F and G to discover new chords. Look at the diagram below. What **similar** chords do you already know?

Chords with Inversions in F Major

R 1st 2nd   R 1st 2nd   R 1st 2nd   R 1st 2nd   R 1st 2nd

R 1st 2nd   R 1st 2nd   R 1st 2nd   R 1st 2nd

Remember to look ahead for fingering

8.1 - PLAYING CHORDS IN F

EXERCISE: Play the following exercises below. Instead of writing R for root, write the **name of the root** below each chord. If the chord is in an inversion, write a slash under the root name and then write the name of the bottom note. The first four chords are done for you.

8.1a

F   F/A   Bb   Bb/D

8.1b

8.1c

8.2 - WRITING CHORDS IN F

Write out the full left hand chord and then play the following root position chords and inversions. (Remember to use the preceeding pages as a guide to writing the correct chord and inversion.

Remember to play each hand separately, then play together.

8.2a

F   F/A   Bb F/A C/G   F/A Bb F/C Bb/D C/E C/G F

8.2b

Bb   F/A F   Bb   F/A Bb/F C/G   C   F

8.2c

F C/G F/A C   F/C C   Bb   C   Bb/D Bb C G/C   F/C   F

8.3 - ROOTS AND INVERSIONS IN G MAJOR

Chords with Inversions in G Major

Like the diagrams in the previous chapters, this diagram outlines the chords in the key of G with the inversions. Do you recognize any of the chords?
(If needed, write the inversions under the name of the chords.)

8.4 - PLAYING CHORDS IN G

EXERCISE: Play the following exercises below. Instead of writing R for root, write the **name of the root** below each chord. If the chord is in an inversion, write a slash under the root name and then write the name of the bottom note. The first four chords are done for you.

8.4a

G   G/D   G   C/G   __   __   __   __

8.4b

8.4c

www.thevirtualschoolofmusic.com

8.5 - WRITING CHORDS IN G

The lowest left hand note is UNDER the slash.

EXERCISE: Write out the full left hand chord and then play the following root position chords and inversions. (Remember to use the preceeding pages as a guide to writing the correct chord and inversions.)

8.5a

G/B G   C   G/B   C   G/D   G   G

8.5b

C   C/E   D   D/F#   G   G/B   D   G

8.5c

D/A   G   D/A   G   C/G   D/F#   G

8.6 - REVIEW EXERCISES

Use your chord diagrams for assistance in completing the exercises.

EXERCISE: Use the chord chart diagrams from Chapter 7 and 8 to create the left hand chords in the following exercises. (The key is written below each exercise.)

8.6a

C:

8.6b

F:

8.6c

G:

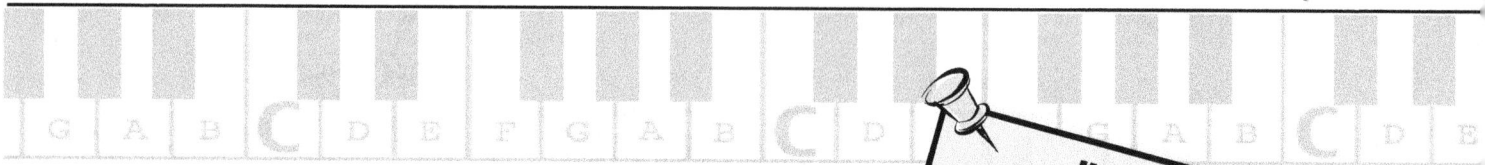

Use full keyboard diagram on page 55 to help with low and high notes

8.6c

G:

8.6d

C:

8.6e

F:

G A B C D E F G A B C D E F G A B C D E

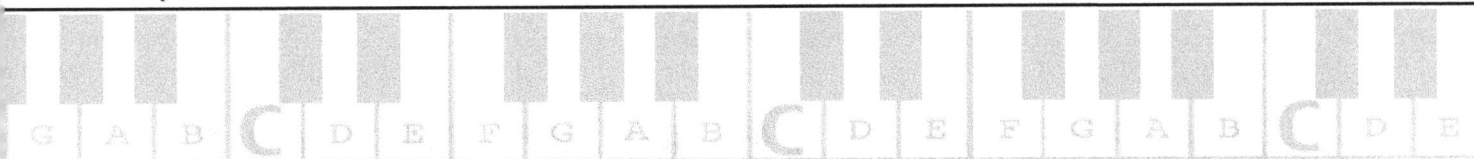

Congratulations!

Now you know how to read basic music notation and
how to determine basic chords and inversions in the left hand.

But, wait... there is still more for you to learn:

• Using your new knowledge, begin to find chordal harmonies
for the melodies you already know
• Start to learn the chords and inversions in new keys
- start with major scales starting on G, F, Bb and D (see pages 56 and 58)
• Begin to write your own melodies and add some simple chords
with their inversions to your melodies

Ready for even more?
See you in Piano for Everyone: Level Two!

ADDITIONAL MATERIALS

A. KEYBOARD LAYOUT

B. CHROMATIC SCALE - TWO OCTAVES

55

C. ALL MAJOR SCALES - TWO OCTAVES

C Major Scale:

F Major Scale:

Bb Major Scale:

Eb Major Scale:

Ab Major Scale:

C. ALL MAJOR SCALES - TWO OCTAVES - CONTINUED

Db Major Scale:

F# Major Scale:

B Major Scale:

E Major Scale:

A Major Scale:

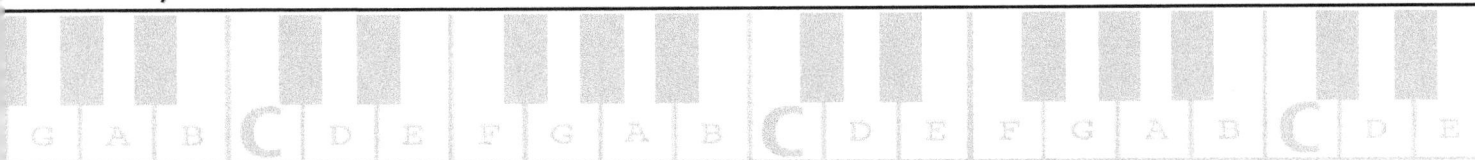

C. MAJOR SCALES - TWO OCTAVES - CONTINUED

D Major Scale:

G Major Scale:

D. CIRCLE OF FIFTHS DIAGRAM

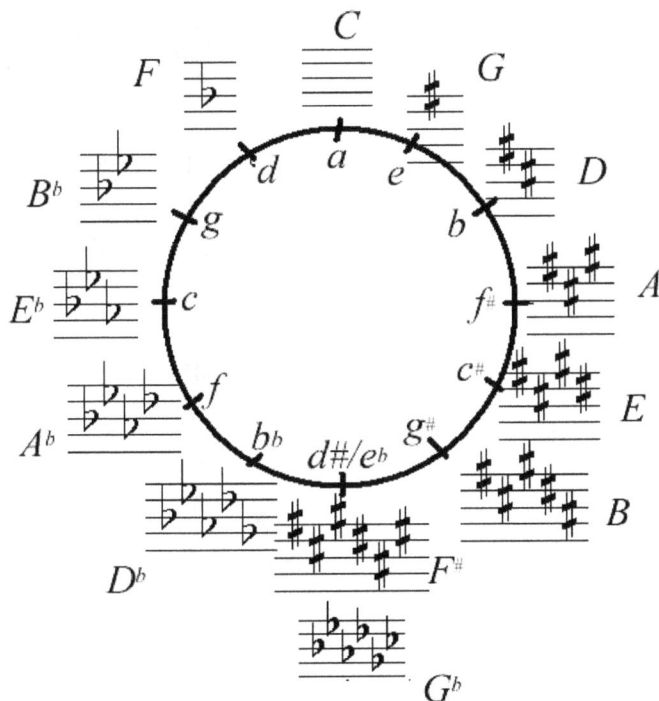

E. SEVENTH CHORD NOMENCLATURE

Major Seventh:

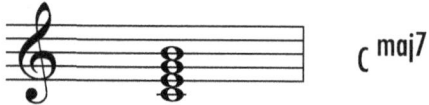 C maj7

Minor Seventh:

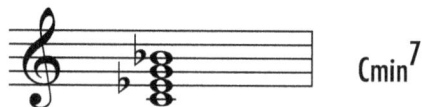 Cmin7

Diminished Seventh:

 C o7

Major-Minor Seventh:

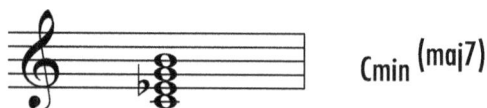 Cmin (maj7)

Major Sixth:

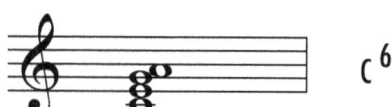 C 6

Sus 4:

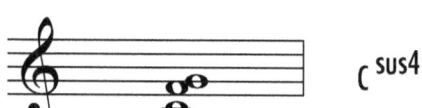 C sus4

Dominant Seventh:

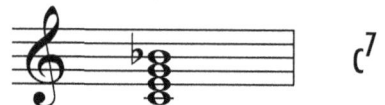 C7

Half Diminished Seventh:

 C ø7 (or Cmin7 b5)

Augmented Seventh:

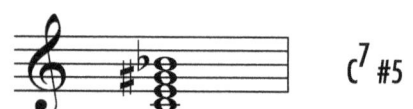 C7 #5

Seven Sus 4:

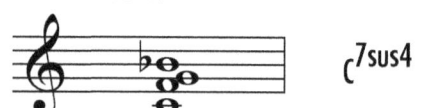 C7sus4

Minor Sixth:

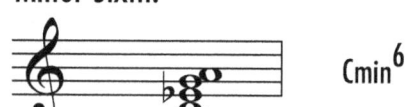 Cmin6

Sus 2:

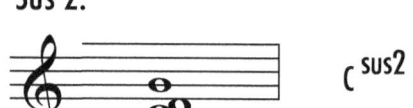 C sus2

Other Resources to Consider:

Classical Piano Works: A Compilation
ISBN 978-1-897515-09-9
This resource contains over 25 classical piano pieces for the beginner piano students through advanced level students. Compiled works include pieces written by Beethoven, Mozart, Schumann and other classical composers.

Music Notes and Rhythms: Volume One by C.A. Johnson and Tamara Baird
ISBN 978-0-9781670-0-4
An introductory music theory methods book for the non-musician, Volume One provides non-music students lesson-by lesson examples and exercises. Lessons teach students to read basic pitch and rhythmic notation of whole notes, half notes, quarter notes, and eighth notes. (Available in English and Spanish)

Saxophone Dexterity by C.A. Johnson
ISBN 978-0-9781670-4-2
A practical method book for assisting beginner through advanced saxophonists in developing technical facility. This method book is arranged so that all levels of students can be challenged through exercises in major and minor scales, dynamics, vibrato, alternate fingerings, and altissimo register. (Available in English and Spanish)

My Music Workbook: for Elementary Students
ISBN 978-1-897515-07-5
My Music Workbook is the perfect resource for the elementary music classroom. The workbook starts with exercises on writing treble clefs on large staves and works through writing rests and notes on varying pitch. Complete with individual classroom exercises for the basic music student, this 30+ page workbook is ideal for students aged 6 - 12 and grade 3 - 6 music classes.

20 Saxophone Etudes and Duets by C.A. Johnson
ISBN 978-0-9781670-5-9
Written by C.A. Johnson, "20 Saxophone Etudes and Duets," contains etudes and duets for the beginner through advanced saxophonists. Challenges in rhythms, time signature, finger movement, and overall technical facility are the focus of this book.

Available online at:
www.thevirtualschoolofmusic.com
info@thevirtualschoolofmusic.com

www.ingramcontent.com/pod-product-compliance
Lightning Source LLC
Chambersburg PA
CBHW080536090426
42733CB00015B/2604